Money Leaves Clues

27 Secrets to Financial Freedom

John S. Rhodes

Copyright © 2013   John S. Rhodes

All rights reserved. No part of this publication may be reproduced, distributed, or transmitted in any form or by any means, including photocopying, recording, or other electronic or mechanical methods, without the prior written permission of the publisher, except in the case of brief quotations embodied in critical reviews and certain other noncommercial uses permitted by copyright law.

Published by JJ Fast Publishing LLC

This book is for my beautiful wife, Megan. It was going to be dedicated to my son, Jackson. However, he just pooped his pants and we're not on good terms right now.

Money Leaves Clues

27 Secrets to Financial Freedom

Table of Contents

INTRODUCTION	9
WHAT IS MONEY?	11
THE SOURCE OF UNLIMITED WEALTH	13
DEBT SUCKS	17
CASH NEVER STOPS TALKING BUT FEW PEOPLE LISTEN	19
THE BEST PLACE TO BE RICH	23
THE ONE THING THAT ALL RICH PEOPLE DO	27
THE FASTEST WAY TO GET MORE MONEY	29
WORK FOR THOUSANDS OF PEOPLE	31
THE BEST WAY TO GENERATE MONEY	33
THE NUMBER ONE SKILL YOU MUST HAVE	37
WHAT YOU MUST FOCUS ON IMMEDIATELY	41
HOW TO KEEP MORE MONEY BY SPENDING IT	43
STOCK INVESTING MADE SIMPLE	45

WHY RICH PEOPLE DON'T CARE ABOUT INCOME TAXES	49
HOW TO PLUG THE "MONEY HOLE" THAT'S DRAINING YOUR BUCKET	53
HOW MONEY GETS FRIED TO A CRISP AND HOW TO STOP IT	57
PICK YOUR POISON	59
HOW TO LIVE LIKE A BILLIONAIRE	61
WHY YOU MUST BE GLOOMY ABOUT PESSIMISM	65
YOU ARE RICH	67

INTRODUCTION

My name is John S. Rhodes people tell me I'm rich. I guess that means I'm rich. But, as far as I'm concerned, I'm just getting started. This is a journey.

When it comes to money I'm kind of strange. I think about cash in weird ways. When I talk about money, and investing, and wealth, I usually get odd looks like I have three heads or something. That doesn't bother me at all. I'm doing just fine. The block of cheese on my shoulders is screwed on well enough.

So, what's this book about and why should you care?

"Money Leaves Clues" is about simple money management and financial freedom. It's a bit philosophical but it's also extremely practical where it matters. It's about creating and keeping wealth. It's what I've done and what I plan on doing until I die. This is about serious money stuff.

In short, if you want to know how to get rich and stay rich, this is for you.

Let's get started

WHAT IS MONEY?

I believe that money is freedom. More money, more freedom.

I believe that money is energy. It represents work, effort and most importantly value. It's a tool that allows me, and you, to exchange three cans pinto beans for two bags of marshmallows.

Money doesn't care about you. Money isn't good, or evil. It doesn't "do" much at all. It's a symbol. It's stored value. And, it's backed only by faith. The faith that tomorrow I can use money to exchange goods and services, and that I can trade my energy for your energy.

I certainly don't worship money. I don't care about the paper or ink. I don't care much about having hundreds of dollars in my money clip. I do care about energy transfer and I do care about the value money represents. Oh yes, and I absolutely pay attention to the faith others place in my cash.

But listen, money isn't wealth. Money is kind of weak and lame. In fact, any old pile of twenty dollar bills decays in value over time due to inflation. Did you know that the U.S. dollar has fallen in value by a mind blowing 86% since 1965? Put that in your pipe and smoke it.

The point is that money isn't your friend or your enemy. Money is not the problem or the solution. Money is like electricity or water. It just lubricates the transfer of value from one person to the next. It's not beautiful, or wonderful or even all that sexy. What you can do with it is what matters.

Of course, you can use this new "Ah ha!" about money to your advantage. One instant trick is to take your money and put it into action. Convert money into an asset, which is something that generates even more money. Your money needs to work for you.

You're going to get clarity on all of this. Just keep reading.

THE SOURCE OF UNLIMITED WEALTH

The best way to make money is by knowing your own skills and then creating value for other people. This will always work and here's the blueprint...

First, make a list of everything you love doing. Second, circle everything on the list that other people will give you money for doing or creating. Finally, rank the items on the list that you've circled according to what will make the most money for you in the fastest time possible. You should probably start doing #1, #2, or #3 (or all three) as soon as possible.

This blueprint will never fail because you will always be doing what you love. You'll have unlimited energy and ridiculous focus. You will never stop. You cannot help but do these things. You only do what you love. And, you will create value.

The blueprint also works because you will only be doing things that people want you to do. You know that because they are giving you money. If you can't make money, then you shouldn't have circled those things. You can't help but make money because every activity you circled on your list creates cash. You provide value, they give you cash.

You will always get freedom and power using this blueprint. You made the list. You looked inside yourself and made the decisions. But, you also looked at the market. You know what people will give you money for doing. You also prioritized the list. So, you know exactly where to start. You know your top priority. Just go do it and get rich.

Up, up and away!

If you ever lose your way, or feel helpless, just use this blueprint again. In fact, you can use it once per day. Or, once per month. Or, once per year. Whenever you want. It always works. It's your new friend. It's also your official source of unlimited wealth.

For the record, this is what I call personality based value creation. Furthermore, this is why I constantly take any new personality test I find. After all, I'm the ultimate weapon and the better I understand myself, the better I understand the weapon.

This blueprint and this process is why I create so many new lists. It's why I dream big and throw my ideas into the market, relentlessly.

This blueprint gives you a wealth creation machine that never stops. Chug, chug, chug.

DEBT SUCKS

Debt makes me sick to my stomach. The problem is that debt gives the other guy all the control and power. I might get something right now because I'm using borrowed money but the other guy gets a lot more money from me.

Debt locks up your future money. When you use debt, you lose the ability to make other choices with your money because it's locked up in payments. And, if you don't pay, you end up in court, you lose your stuff and the dog growls at you.

Debt is an obligation. It's a dark cloud over your life. Debt locks you into the service of other people. Debt forces you to work. So, your decision to go into debt is a decision to make future payments to other people. It makes others rich.

The key here is that debt is your decision. When you take on debt, you're making the conscious and deliberate decision to give other people your money, so that you can have something right now. You're trading freedom for cash. That's debt.

Should you take on debt for education? Probably, but you should probably minimize your school debt as much possible. Should you take on debt for a new home? Sure, if that house you're buying is well below market value and you're going to flip it, or it's a dream home at a fair price, or that sort of thing. Should you take on debt to buy a new pair of shoes? Probably not.

Debt is the result of your decision to make other people rich. And, make no mistake; the people selling you money are extremely good at making you feel like you're getting a wonderful deal. But, dig deeper and it becomes pretty obvious lenders are the winners.

Debt is the big fail.

CASH NEVER STOPS TALKING BUT FEW PEOPLE LISTEN

There's a running joke in my house. It seems that I keep buying the same book over and over because when my wife asks me if I'm learning anything new, I tell her no.

Here's why: I read a lot of books about business, investing and success. It's the same stuff over and over. I'm rarely shocked by a new business idea or success story.

Here's what I've learned. You get wealthy by working hard. Most millionaires are self-made, frugal and own their own businesses. You make money by delivering value to people and by helping them be successful. You must be generous. Get focused and never give up. And, so on.

I see this stuff in action. My successful friends are relentless. They are genuine. They are caring, honest and open. My business partners are focused. They have written goals. They know what they want and they just go get it. Money is attracted to them.

Success requires focused work that creates value. Money will tell you to put in extra time and effort to deliver great products in the market. You can literally look at a market and see the success if you look at the products and services, but more importantly, how those products and services were created. There's quality. There's real value.

Here's something you can do right now, if you want to take action. Just start asking wealthy people what works. Find mentors. Find coaches. And, when you do, pay them a ton of money, if they will take it. There's nothing better than paying for instant access to the success pipeline. Money talks when you use it. Money talks if you ask it to speak.

If you don't know wealthy and successful people, just take a look at the long term winners in your market. What advertisements show up again and again, over years and years? What products keep selling, no matter what? What kinds of people get on top and stay on top?

Be relentless about finding these clues and driving them into your skull again and again, from different angles, with different stories and through different people. You need to listen to all the different voices money uses. Money is your friend but money can be shy so you have to listen carefully.

Want another shortcut? Every successful person I know reads a lot of books. Furthermore, they are always testing and experimenting. Wealthy people are learning machines and they never stop listening to what money is saying. Reading is the best shortcut in the world.

THE BEST PLACE TO BE RICH

Wealth creation starts and ends in your own home. I'm not talking about real estate, although that is one path to a huge fortune. I'm talking about getting rich and staying rich by treating your household like a business.

Sounds stuffy. Sounds boring. Sounds like a pain. But, it's a lot easier than you might think. I'll explain how to do it in 4 steps.

First, write down all the sources of money flowing into your house. This is your revenue. Second, write down all the money flowing out of your house each month. These are your expenses. If you subtract these expenses from the revenue coming in, you now understand net profit. That's what you've got left over.

The third step is writing down everything that you owe. These are your debts. Fourth, you write down everything that gives you money back every month. Stocks, bonds, savings account, 401K. Stuff like that. These are your assets.

By the way, I'm weird in that I don't count my house as an asset because it costs me money to own every single month. I don't count cars, either. They drain cash too. They wear out. So,

I'm really strict about my assets. I only track the stuff that increases in value over time and throws off cash.

Now, the last step is simple. If you want to get rich do the following. Increase revenue and decrease expenses. This is like eating less and exercising more. Take any extra cash and either kill off your debt or add to your assets. Keep track of what you're doing, month after month.

You need to track your net worth. Wealth is all about what you keep. Profit is important but it's how you take that profit and use it to increase wealth that matters. You can track your net worth with a paper and pencil. That's how I got started. Today I use a spreadsheet with data that I've tracked month-to-month for more than 6 years. It's a hot and sexy spreadsheet. It tells a beautiful story.

They say that what you focus on grows. Although I track income, I pay more attention to my net worth because it's net worth that determines your wealth, not income.

In summary, track money in, money out, money you owe and money you keep. Once you've done this for about 3 months your life will change because you will feel the pain of money leaving your life and you'll be thrilled when your net income increases. These emotions are fuel to keep you focused on the growth of your wealth. This is easy, too.

THE ONE THING THAT ALL RICH PEOPLE DO

Every rich person that I know reads a lot. Typically, the greatest focus is on what generates the most wealth for that person. Wealthy people are attracted to topics such as self-improvement, investing, and personal success. They also tend to read as a habit but also for enjoyment.

This totally makes sense. You are what you read. If you fill your mind and heart with ideas, tools and systems related to success and building wealth, you can't help but get more successful. Getting rich becomes natural and expected. It becomes very normal to make more money and keep more money.

But, it's really about more than reading. Getting rich is a state of mind. It's a way of viewing the world.

All wealthy individuals act in the present but constantly plan for the future, delivering value now and always. Wealth is also more about producing value for others and using energy to make life better for others. Wealth becomes a side effect of being awesome.

So, again, rich people live in the here and now. But, they think in terms of abundance and a greater future. Books help. Talking to other rich people helps. But, it's the current focus and future thinking that characterizes the wealth mindset.

Your mind and your attitude get you rich now. Your future mind keeps you rich. You need to take care of both, at the same time. Focus on too much on the "now" and greed boils in your veins. Focus too much on the future and you become an envious dreamer. The rich and powerful know how to balance the forces.

THE FASTEST WAY TO GET MORE MONEY

If you want to make money really fast then help a lot of other people make a lot of money as fast as possible. Help other people get rich quick. This is the way to get money for yourself extremely fast and you can do this again and again. It's a proven success formula.

The reason this works is very simple: When you help others make money, they will give you a piece of the action. And, if you help a lot of people make a lot of money, you get lots of pieces of a lot of pies. Add them up and your total pie is pretty damn big.

I'll explain this a different way. I often talk about production versus consumption. If you produce more than you consume, you will get rich over time. You get rich faster by writing and selling books than reading books. You get rich faster by selling lemonade than drinking lemonade. And, so on. Produce more than you consume. Create more value than you chew up.

The key here is creating value, not just doing work for the sake of work. You get paid for value. Apply some energy to help other people get what they want and you will win the game.

You can do this again and again. It's foolproof. It's liberating.

A great example is when you help people turn a hobby into a part-time or full-time income. Maybe you know something about brewing beer. You know how to make an extra $500 per month brewing and selling beer. That's great! But, the real wealth explosion comes from showing 100 people how to make $500 per month. That training can be sold to those 100 people for maybe $100, which means you just made $10,000 helping 100 people. That's 20 times the amount of money you'd make just brewing and selling your own beer. And, you capture that cash extremely fast. It would take you 20 months to make that much that fast, selling your own beer.

Don't just make money. Show a lot of other people how to make a lot of money. Even a small fraction of their wealth creation gives you stacks of cash.

The lesson is to help other people achieve their dreams, demand a fair price for helping them, and get wealthy a lot faster. It is the fastest way to get rich.

WORK FOR THOUSANDS OF PEOPLE

If you have a day job and work for someone else, you have just one customer. What I mean is that your job is tied to one company. If your boss doesn't like you and you get fired, then you go from 100% employment to 0% employment instantly. Or, if the company goes belly up, you go from making cash to making nothing. Full stop.

Your job, and the business behind it, is equivalent to having just one customer. There is a single point of failure in your financial life. The fear and dread you feel in your gut about your job is a direct result of knowing that every day, your financial security is on the line. It's all or nothing.

Freaked out yet? Understand the risk?

Well, I have a simple solution for you. You need 1,000 customers. If one customer doesn't like you, so what? You only have a loss of 1% (or less) of your income. Big deal!

Now, I can read your mind. You're wondering how to get 1,000 or more customers. The answer is that you need to start and run your own business. You need to be an entrepreneur. That's the secret of the rich.

(More than 2/3 of all millionaires are self employed.)

The crazy thing about having your own business with hundreds or thousands of customers is that your financial risk is substantially lower than just having a job with one employer. You're at the mercy of an employer if you have a job. But, with a big, fat pile of customers, you have unlimited lifeblood. You have money just waiting to flow your way. You can roll with the punches again and again.

The bottom line is that you've been brainwashed into thinking that your day job is safer than running your own business. The greatest financial asset you can have is a giant list of happy customers with a pipeline of groovy products. That is power and freedom.

THE BEST WAY TO GENERATE MONEY

You want your money to asexually reproduce. Asexual money reproduction is the process by which money grows and copies itself. You don't need to lift a finger.

Sounds impossible, but it's not.

It's done with compound interest. As Einstein says, compound interest is the greatest mathematical discovery of all time. Start with $50,000, add 8% compound interest on that $50,000 over 40 years and end up with $1,086,226.07. Or, start with $25,000, add 10% compound interest over 40 years and get $1,131,481.39. So, start with 50% less money, add just 2% more, and you get to over a million dollars.

I'm sure if you're reading this, you've seen these kinds of numbers before. I've learned that saving money like crazy is essential. Frugality is a secret weapon. Even a small amount of extra cash gives you the seed money for compounding. I've also learned to seek out higher returns with lower risk.

Really, compound interest depends on just two factors. First, the initial capital and second, the rate of interest. It also means that taking money out kills the machine. You need to save money, get it asexually reproducing through compound interest and leave it alone. Reinvest the money and don't mess with the machine. It's critical to leave the principle and the interest alone. Put money in and never take it out.

So, how do you increase the initial "seed nut" of capital? Simple! Start a business. It can be a full-time business or it can be part-time business. There's no faster and ethical way to make money.

You can increase your rate of interest, or your rate of return, by investing in the stock market the right way. If you're wondering, I follow the principles laid out by folks like Ben Graham, Warren Buffett, Phil Fisher and other old time value investors. I diversify but I also flow my own money into low price but high quality companies. If I'm feeling stupid then I just add money to one of my super low cost, broadly diversified index funds. If I'm feeling smart and I've done my research, then I load up on an individual stock like crazy.

I will boil all this down into a rather simple formula. First, work for yourself. Start a business. Take the extra money the business generates and plow it back into the business. Or, drop that extra cash it into the stock market using a cheap index fund or drop it into undervalued but high quality stocks, with the expectation that you can't touch that money for a long time.

THE NUMBER ONE SKILL YOU MUST HAVE

I went to school for 10 years. I have an Associate's degree. I have a Bachelor's degree. And, I have two Masters degrees. This might make you think that I think that education is really important. Well, it's true. I think having an education is essential.

That said, I do not believe that having advanced degrees is essential. I think it's pretty smart to have a college education as a matter of insurance. It can help if you need to get a job. However, what really matters is the education, not the college degree.

Furthermore, you must become a lifelong learner. You need to be hungry for more information, more training and more knowledge. If you want to get rich and be rich, you've got to be a learning machine. That's because even if you earn a bunch of money, you probably won't be able to keep it as the world changes around you.

(Many high income earners know how to make... and burn money.)

All human interaction requires persuasion. All communication is about sales and selling, in one fashion or another. Never forget that.

Here's how Dan Sullivan explains sales and selling:

Selling is the act of getting somebody intellectually and emotionally committed to a future result that is good for them and then getting them to commit to take action.

So, you need to communicate and interact. You need to get logic and emotions engaged. You need a focus on the future with positive results. You need to cause action, with strong commitment backing the action.

We are all sales people. It's the number one "money skill" you can get but it's also one of the best life skills you can improve. Sell, sell, sell.

Remember this, too: What you focus on grows. If you want the skill of selling, you must focus on the skill. And, you must do it your entire life. You'll never reach perfection in selling but every small fraction of improvement provides enormous financial leverage.

(p.s. I love copywriting.)

WHAT YOU MUST FOCUS ON IMMEDIATELY

One of the amazing things that I've read about and that I've seen firsthand is that many rich people have a hard time staying rich. Obviously, there are plenty of wealthy people who stay wealthy and get even wealthier. But, like those ill-fated lottery winners who make it and lose it, many people who become rich have a hard time staying rich.

The reason is simple. Most people are focused on making money. They get better and better at making money. They are focused on income. However, the "losers" never focus on how to keep their money once they have it. And, they don't know how to grow the money they make hand over fist. One the other hand, the real "winners" focus on building wealth and forcing their money to grow without work.

There is a secret to increasing your income and keeping then growing your wealth...

This is extremely simple. It's shockingly easy. You just need to track your wealth. No joke, that's it. Set aside about 10-15 minutes each month to review your net worth which is the pile of cash that you have after all expenses have been paid and after you subtract out all your debt.

Your 10-15 minute "job" each month is to monitor your net worth. Remember, what you focus on grows. So, by tracking your net worth, your net worth will grow. You'll get smarter and smarter about cutting expenses. You'll realize that debt is dragging you down. You'll learn ways to make the pile of cash grow faster with lower risk. Awesome stuff like that. The rich and powerful closely watch their net worth.

The secret is to think about all the money that you get to keep, not about the money that you are making. Watch the money flow in but more importantly learn to use that money to kill off debt and increase your assets which throw off cash and grow over time.

Track your net worth! (Even if it's negative. Get to breakeven. Then, keep going.)

HOW TO KEEP MORE MONEY BY SPENDING IT

If you want to get rich you've got to spend money. But, you've got to spend money like rich people, or you'll get poorer fast.

When I use the word "spend" I'm talking about it differently than most people. I'm talking about allocating capital. I'm talking about moving money from Point A to Point B. When you spend money you are making a decision about where it goes and how it's used. When you spend $100 you're deciding on the particular purpose of that $100. Spending money is a decision making activity. It's a conscious activity.

So, if you want to make and keep more money then you simply need to spend it on things that grow your income and net worth. It's that simple. You need to spend money on debt reduction. You need to spend money on assets which grow in value and spit out cash, like stocks and real estate. You need to spend money to grow income and grow net worth.

You can really zero in here by thinking about how you use your money. If you buy a candy bar you're not creating or growing an asset. You're growing your waistline but not your wealth. On the other hand, if you spend money on a real estate investment you're getting an asset that throws off cash and you're getting an asset that grows in value over time due to its ability to throw off even more cash in the future. You're spending money to get even more future money.

For the record, very few rich people sit on piles of cash. They spend their money. They invest in their businesses, in real estate, in stocks, in bonds and so forth. They spend money to acquire assets. They spend money to kill debt. Wealthy people stay rich though smart allocation of money. They spend their money the right way. Every dollar you spend is a vote to get richer or poorer.

STOCK INVESTING MADE SIMPLE

I don't gamble. I don't trade commodities. I don't speculate. Instead, I invest my money for the long haul. My time horizon is buy and hold forever. Of course, I buy and sell stocks but I do it with the intention of holding my stocks for extremely long periods. This keeps my commissions low and it keeps me focused on picking great stocks.

I could write an entire book on my stock picking process. Although it's pretty simple, the philosophical foundation is absolutely critical to understand. I'd spend most of the pages in that book explaining all the reasons why each little piece of my stock picking process makes sense, and why it works so well.

All that said, great stock investing is surprisingly simple. Before I explain the ultra simple process I'll give you a few facts. This is based on my own experience but more importantly, extensive research and reading about stock market success. You can verify this stuff yourself if you like what I'm cooking here.

First, you need to realize that you're probably going to lose a lot of money if you pick individual stocks on your own unless you are ridiculously dedicated and focused. You have to enjoy it and you have to treat it as more than a mere hobby. It's deadly serious work so you have to love it to stick with it over a long period of time.

And, you'll still probably lose.

Second, most stock professionals and mutual fund managers fail to beat the market. More than 90% of all mutual fund managers will not beat the market over 5 years. Even the pros are terrible, but they are great at taking your money. In short, it's hard to beat the market but it's surprisingly easy to match the market.

So, now that you're a little bit freaked out, here's the system that I use that works. It's so dumb and simple that you'll love it. What you need to do is invest in no load, ultra low cost index funds that track a broad market. Examples include Vanguard's Total Stock Market Index Fund, Schwab's Total Stock Market Index Fund and Fidelity's Spartan Total Market Index Fund. They all have expense ratios below 0.20% percent. That means they aren't stealing a bunch of cash from you each year.

Some "actively managed" mutual funds will charge you fees upwards of 5%. They will cost you 5 times to 25 times as much money as a simple index fund. They are borderline thieves. So, go passive and avoid active money management. Those mutual fund money managers are mostly a bunch of clowns. *Honk, honk!*

That's really it. You can buy books about investing but this is the smartest way to go in my experience and based on all my research. A huge of amount of my own net worth is invested in stocks through these zero load, low cost index funds. The rest of my stock market money is invested in stocks that I've carefully selected over time based on proven "old school" principles explained by guys like Ben Graham, Warren Buffett and Phil Fisher. That stuff works, plain and simple. But, it's not glamorous or instant. It's time consuming and tedious. I'm a glutton for this kind of punishment so I love it. Most people throw up even thinking about this kind of research.

The bottom line is that it's wicked hard to beat the market. So, don't fight that. Join the entire market at the lowest possible cost. It's smart, it's easy. It works.

WHY RICH PEOPLE DON'T CARE ABOUT INCOME TAXES

I care about taxes. I bet you care about taxes. Rich people care about taxes, too. However, the rich don't really care much about income taxes. Instead, they care about the taxes that actually impact them.

Think about how you are taxed. You make money and the government takes their slice. Your income is taxed. Your revenue is taxed. For every dollar you make, you lose some to the government. The income gets redistributed to the common good and directly to special interests and entitlements. That's how it works and that's how it'll probably always work.

However, there's a "glitch" in the system. Or, maybe a "loophole" that the rich enjoy. Although high income earners like stockbrokers, doctors, lawyers and others like them care about income taxes, most wealthy people care more about keeping the money they've already got in their hands, not about the money that flows in from a job.

That's essential to understand. People focused on income and revenue and their paychecks are focused on income taxes. But, people focused on their wealth and their net worth care about taxes on capital gains and dividends. They care about the taxes on their wealth and less about the taxes on their income.

Most people focus the taxes associated with income flow. This gives wealthy people a wonderful advantage. Their wealth remains hidden. What I mean is that dividends and long term capital gains typically have lower tax rates than straight income. Income tax rates in the U.S. right now range from 15% to 39.6% while long term capital gains are 15-20% and dividends are 15%. In other words, taxes on income are higher than taxes on income spit out by wealth.

What does all this mean? In simple terms, it means that you want to ethically and legally reduce your income taxes as much as you can but that you also want to get your money working for you using assets that grow. Once again, the best way to get rich and minimize your tax burden is to start your own company, invest in stocks and real estate. That's a simplification but it's an important simplification. Do what the rich do, play the game that the rich play.

By the way, this "tax thing" is exactly why it's so smart to buy and hold great stocks for a long time. If you buy a stock it can grow and grow but you don't get taxed as it grows, except for dividends. There's much less tax friction to slow you down if you buy and hold. Every time you buy and sell there's another cut to your wealth due to the "little knives" of transaction costs and capital gains taxes. The more you trade stocks, the more you chew up your money. Turnover kills you. You're taxed when you take action. Patience drives your taxes lower.

In short, income is not wealth. Income is what your wealth creates for you. Taxes are high on income but they are much lower on wealth accumulation. That's what the rich are doing to gain more freedom and power.

HOW TO PLUG THE "MONEY HOLE" THAT'S DRAINING YOUR BUCKET

This is the best way to understand how your money dies. It's easy to prevent money death but you have to understand how it happens first, then you can stop it.

First, if you don't keep more than spend, you're totally sunk. You can easily plug the hole in the ship by delaying gratification. In other words, before you buy something, just wait. Wait a day. Wait a month. Wait a year. The longer you wait the better chance you have of decreasing your debt and increasing your assets.

This is a weapon of long term wealth!

Wealthy people are almost always frugal people. They rarely kill their money. Instead, they are cautious and careful about every dime that comes in and goes out.

Years ago I remember telling my friend Danny that I needed new sneakers. He told me to go buy them if I needed them. But, I told him that I was going to wait just one more month before buying them. I told him that by doing this, I would save on the cost of 5-6 pairs of sneakers over my lifetime. Now, trust me, I know this seems utterly ridiculous. It sounds nuts. But, I'm talking about waiting just one extra month to buy those new sneakers. Doing this will plow hundreds of dollars back into my net worth over my life. And, I still get the sneakers I want but it just takes a little bit longer.

Rich people think differently.

The point of the story above is that by waiting just a little while before spending your money, you generate hundreds of extra dollars of extra net worth per month. I delay gratification on virtually all spending. The "pain" of waiting is minimal and all of that extra money is plowed back into my assets which continue to grow, which just generates that much extra money that I can spend later.

Delayed gratification from years ago is now paying me back in a huge way right now. All that money saved from years ago just keeps on growing and growing, doing a lot of work for me. It won't stop asexually reproducing.

The trick is just waiting a little bit longer for what you want. Stop your emotional juices from flowing so you don't buy what you don't really want or need. Use some logic to make a smarter decision by waiting a little while longer. This waiting decreases the chances of wasting money on what you don't really want or need and it increases the chances that your money will grow more through compound interest and asset appreciation.

You can start delaying gratification immediately. It's like a muscle. You need to exercise it to make it stronger.

HOW MONEY GETS FRIED TO A CRISP AND HOW TO STOP IT

What happens when you make $100? It's simple, right? The $100 comes in and then you drop it in your bank account or your pocket. Then, you buy stuff. Sometimes, you need more than $100 and you drop the purchase on a credit card. You end up with less than $100 and you're in debt, and frustrated.

Let's stop that. First, always plan on "paying yourself" first. Take a fraction of every $100 and put it into savings or a low cost no load stock index fund. Or, pay down your debt. Do this again and again, and you will start to get rich as long as you don't spend more than you're investing.

Time to get specific. You've got four quadrants that matter. First, money in (revenue), then money out (expenses), then money burned on fun stuff (discretionary spending) and finally, money saved (asset growth).

$100 comes in. You must spend $90 to buy groceries, pay rent, pay for the car, pay down credit card debt, pay for student loans, or whatever. That leaves you with $10 more to spend. This is where things get interesting. You can go crazy and invest the entire $10 or at the other extreme you can burn the $10 on video games, movies, flowers for your wife, dog toys, Godiva chocolates or whatever else suits your fancy. Or, you can balance things out. You can invest $7 and burn $3. Or, vice versa. If you chose to spend all $10 then you will not get rich. On the other hand, if you invest all $10 then you'll probably be frustrated, burned out and dull. The key is to invest as much of the remaining $10 while having some fun in the sun.

Now, you might argue that it's smarter to focus on increasing the $100. Or, that it's smarter to decrease your expenses. I won't argue about this. What matters is that you know the four quadrants and that you focus on constantly plowing money into your investments, your assets and your business while reducing expenses and having a bit of fun. Money gets killed when you do not track and monitor money moving into and between the four quadrants.

The secret is that you need to know how your money is flowing in and flowing out. You have to make a choice to get rich by taking any extra money and putting it into your net worth. Reduce debt, increase assets. But, have fun. Get naked once in a while. If you follow any other path you will fry your money just like an ant under a magnifying glass on a hot sunny day.

PICK YOUR POISON

This is so weird and strange that I don't understand it at all. I can only guess that it's some bizarre karma thing. But, again, I don't claim to understand how it works. I only know that it does work.

I'm talking about being generous and caring. I'm talking about donating time and money to other people. And, I know from personal experience that the more that I give away the more that I make. It doesn't make sense but it's true.

There's a catch, however. When you give and donate and help, you simply cannot do it out of greed or with any expectation of reciprocation or getting anything in return. You have to just do it because it feels good and because you want to make the world a better place. If you expect something in return, it doesn't work.

Fortunately, helping other people is awesome. It's fun. It's entertaining. It's wonderful. So, you get rewarded just for doing the right thing and you don't need any money in return. But, the side effect is there. Wealth increases as you give more and more away, and as you help more and more people.

If you aren't donating money or donating your time, or both, start immediately. Not to get wealthy but because it's awesome. And, because there's a good chance that your wealth will increase even faster. That's the icing on the cake. Do it with an open heart and have a blast.

Be generous in a way that works for you. But, be generous. The longer you hold back, the longer you have to wait to get rewarded with smiles and happy vibes from humanity. Although I'm not exactly Mr. Sunshine, I get great pleasure out of helping other people. And, even when some people don't agree with me or frustrate me, I can always feel good about how much I'm able to help others.

Sidebar: I recently learned this lesson from my daughter: When you fill the buckets of other people you are also filling your own bucket. The more love you pour out of your bucket for other people the more your bucket just keeps filling up.

HOW TO LIVE LIKE A BILLIONAIRE

I live like a billionaire. I'm not joking. I'm going to explain exactly how you can live like a billionaire, too. It is surprisingly easy.

First, you have to think about what it would be like to be a billionaire. Basically, you have unlimited money and you can buy whatever you want. You can also go wherever you want, for the most part. But, you can't be at Disney World and Paris at the same time. There are physical limits.

It's extremely important to understand that it's almost impossible spend your way to perpetual happiness. All of the research shows this. Sure, it would be a blast to have a billion dollars and it would be fun to spend it, for a while. But, there are limits to happiness based on raw spending.

What's more important is that every human has limits. For example, we all face death. We all have just 24 hours per day. We all need to sleep. We all need to eat. We all need to poop. It's this awareness of the human condition that gives us a wonderful opportunity.

If you want to spend 1/3 of your time sleeping like a billionaire just invest in an excellent bed and sheets. Even the very best bed and high thread count sheets will set you back just a few thousand dollars. So, for less than $5,000 you can spend 1/3 of your time living just like a billionaire. Zzzzzz.

Taking this idea several steps ahead, you can spend very little money to enjoy small but extremely significant luxuries. For example, you can buy super high quality toilet paper. I know that sounds funny because it *is* funny. It's also true. Billionaires have to poop and you can use toilet paper as good as theirs, if not better.

Embrace the billionaire lifestyle...

There are so many small, affordable luxuries that give you access to the lifestyle of the rich and powerful. Hours and hours of your life can be spent living exactly like a billionaire. You now have a proven formula!

We live in a world of incredible wealth and luxury. You can make $42,738 per year and still live just like a billionaire for many hours of the day. That's pretty groovy.

The point here really is that it's your state of mind and perspective that give you the opportunity to live a life of luxury. And, when you add in the opportunities that you have to see your family, enjoy your kids and be with your friends, it's impossible to be depressed about all your true wealth.

WHY YOU MUST BE GLOOMY ABOUT PESSIMISM

It's easy to be negative. It's easy to complain. But, surprisingly, life keeps getting better. Less disease, more money per capita, better technology. There are many reasons for this and optimism is finally getting some traction in our culture.

Just consider technology alone. In the last 40-50 years alone we've seen everything from the MP3 player and cell phones to in-vitro fertilization and smoke detectors. The rate of innovation is staggering and capitalism, with all of its faults and problems, allows for the development of incredible wealth. It's up to you to get your hands on it.

If you're totally undecided about how you're going to get rich then consider jumping into technology. But, don't create technology for the sake of technology. Instead, the real secret is that you want to look for ways to use technology to help other people get what they want. Losing weight. Feeling younger. Living longer. Stuff like that never goes out of style. In other words, apply technology in a way that helps other people solve the problems they face.

People are also desperate to find meaning. They want focus. They want freedom and power and control. They want to eat jelly donuts to lose weight but they also want deep, meaningful connections with other people. Tap into these evergreen desires. These are factory installed in all humans. Use technology to drill oil.

But wait, there's more –

If you're trying to figure out how to make money even faster, then you need to specialize. That doesn't mean you should focus 100% of your effort on one thing. You might be inspired by ideas from some very unexpected places. What I mean is that if you zero in on one problem and then you solve that one problem, your chances of success go up substantially. Furthermore, you can fail faster. It takes a lot of failures to hit the homeruns. There will be one pitch after another. Just keep swinging.

YOU ARE RICH

You must believe you are wealthy and that you are getting wealthier every single day. It needs to be cooked into your brain. It must be a fact in your mind.

You're just building on the wealth you already have. There's a lot of money out there with your name on it. You just need to collect what is already yours.

The formula is simple. First, clearly understand that you are already rich. You might not completely feel rich but you *are* rich. You're wealthy. This is a fact. Second, to unlock the wealth you just need to create value for other people. You need to help other people get their hands on their wealth. Third, after you deliver incredible value to other people, collect the money with your name written on it from those people you've helped.

You are rich. Now, just deliver massive value to other people then collect what's yours. Do that repcatcdly. Make it a habit and watch your wealth grow rapidly. This is how you will change the world. This is the freedom and power of the rich. This is the freedom and power that is yours. Embrace it.

www.ingramcontent.com/pod-product-compliance
Lightning Source LLC
Chambersburg PA
CBHW071632170526

45166CB00003B/1297